HERE

&

THERE

Advent reflections
from two cultures

Jill Baker

HERE AND THERE

Week Four – The 'plane now landing

INTRODUCTION

For most children growing up in Britain, the days of Advent are marked by the opening of small cardboard doors in an Advent Calendar. I vividly remember how the excitement mounted as we approached the bigger door marked '24' . . . (sometimes given away by its dog-eared appearance that someone had peeped!). Then Advent candles were 'invented' and people like me, loving lights shining in the darkness were further entranced. Later I discovered Delia Smith's devotional book *A Feast for Advent* and my daily marking of this special season was spiritually enriched.

Coming to live in the Caribbean as a Mission Partner in January 1994 changed much in my life – not least the celebration of Advent and Christmas. None of the children in the Sunday School in Chateaubelair had ever seen an Advent Calendar; lighting candles in church on the four Sundays in Advent was a disaster as the tropical 'Christmas breeze' extinguished them or, if not, blew wax everywhere. Advent was a little-marked season, and I missed the build-up to Christmas I had come to love.

Here and There is a response to that situation, born really out of a desire to travel the road through Advent in the company of friends from 'here' in the Caribbean and 'there' in the UK, to swap our stories and our understandings as we make the pilgrimage together, learning from each other.

Obviously, one or more readings from the final week may have to be omitted depending on where Christmas Day falls in the week. There are enough readings here for the longest possible Advent – ie four full weeks.

Whether you are 'here' or 'there', may God bless you in Advent.

Jill Baker
St George's, Grenada
November 1999

Week One – Waiting

Advent Sunday: What time?

> Do not fret because of the wicked; do not be envious
>   of wrongdoers,
> for they will soon fade like the grass, and wither like
>   the green herb.
> Trust in the Lord and do good; so you will live in the
>   land, and enjoy security.
> Take delight in the Lord, and he will give you the
>   desires of your heart.
> Commit your way to the Lord; trust in him,
>   and he will act.
> He will make your vindication shine like the light,
> and the justice of your cause like the noonday.
> Be still before the Lord, and wait patiently for him;
> do not fret over those who prosper in their way,
> over those who carry out evil devices.
>
> *Psalm 37:1-7*

It was Easter Monday and we were invited to a church barbecue in a nearby village. 'What time?' my husband Andrew asked. 'Five o'clock,' came the answer. We had been living in the Caribbean for about four months and thought we knew all about 'Caribbean Time' so, daringly as it seemed to our Western minds, we didn't set off from home until 5.30pm. On reaching the church fifteen minutes later we met one of the organisers just setting off in his pick-up. He wound down the window and called, 'I'm just off to collect the barbecue drum – see you soon!' It was well after dark when we and our boys – aged then four and a half years and six months – had our supper.

Waiting is a central theme in these weeks of Advent – our children 'can't wait' for Christmas morning, and as Christians we share with the prophets in their waiting and longing for the Messiah. At the same time we are straining forward to the end of all things, waiting for the return of our Lord Jesus Christ.

Living in the Caribbean has taught me just a little about waiting. Waiting need not be a negative waste of time, but can become a positive good as we learn a stillness, a trust, a patience. Psalm 37 exhorts us to a life of patience and trust: 'do not fret . . . trust in the Lord . . . take delight in the Lord . . . commit your way to the Lord . . . trust in him . . . be still before the Lord, and wait patiently for him.'

A prayer:

> *I may have to spend time waiting today, Lord. Thank you that you will be with me even as I wait. Teach me to wait for you and, as I wait, to trust, to be patient, not to fret. Amen.*

Week One — Waiting

Monday: Sarah is promised a son

God said to Abraham, 'As for Sarah your wife, you shall not call her Sarai, but Sarah shall be her name. I will bless her, and moreover I will give you a son by her. I will bless her, and she shall give rise to nations; kings of people shall come from her.' Then Abraham fell on his face and laughed, and said to himself, 'Can a child be born to a man who is a hundred years old? Can Sarah, who is ninety years old, bear a child?' And Abraham said to God, 'O that Ishmael might live in your sight!' God said, 'No, but your wife Sarah shall bear you a son, and you shall name him Isaac. I will establish my covenant with him as an everlasting covenant for his offspring after him. As for Ishmael, I have heard you: I will bless him and make him fruitful and exceedingly numerous; he shall be the father of twelve princes, and I will make him a great nation. But my covenant I will establish with Isaac, whom Sarah shall bear to you at this season next year.' And when he had finished talking with him, God went up from Abraham.

Genesis 17:15-22

Many women have to wait for pregnancy and childbirth — conception doesn't always happen just when we want it to — but not many have had to wait like Sarah waited! At thirty years old when my first child was born I was the oldest in the ante-natal class by some years — Sarah probably wouldn't have shown up for class at all! The years allotted to other characters from the early books of the Bible do suggest that the average life-span was somewhat different in Abraham's day. According to Genesis 23:1 Sarah lived to be 127 years old, so would have seen the son of her old age grow into manhood. However, Abraham's reaction (v17) shows that it was not normal for women of Sarah's age to be having their first babies. How did she cope? I often wonder.

Maybe we can learn from Sarah's story that God operates on a different time-scale from ours. So many of our problems are caused because we can't wait for God's timing. Even Abraham and Sarah fell into this trap, trying to fulfil God's promise (Genesis 15:3-5) by their own methods, resulting in much unhappiness for themselves as well as for poor Hagar and Ishmael (Genesis 16).

I believe that God gives the answer 'wait' to many of our prayers, not because he wants us to suffer or go without, but because he knows, far better than I have yet realised, the value of waiting. You want your children to wait for those Christmas goodies, don't you?

A prayer:

> *Lord God, are you telling me to wait for something today? Help me, Lord, to hear your voice, to have faith in your promises, and to accept that your timing is perfect. Amen.*

Tuesday: Caleb realises his inheritance

Then the people of Judah came to Joshua at Gilgal; and Caleb, son of Jephunneh the Kenizzite said to him, 'You know what the Lord said to Moses the man of God in Kadesh-Barnea concerning you and me. I was forty years old when Moses the servant of the Lord sent me from Kadesh-Barnea to spy out the land; and I brought him an honest report. But my companions who went up with me made the heart of the people melt; yet I wholeheartedly followed the Lord my God. And Moses swore on that day saying, "Surely the land on which your foot has trodden shall be an inheritance for you and your children forever, because you have wholeheartedly followed the Lord my God." And now, as you see, the Lord has kept me alive, as he said, these forty-five years since the time that the Lord spoke this word to Moses, while Israel was journeying through the wilderness; and here I am today, eighty-five years old. I am still as strong today as I was on the day that Moses sent me; my strength now is as my strength was then, for war and for going and coming. So now give me this hill country of which the Lord spoke on that day; for you heard on that day how the Anakim were there, with great fortified cities; it may be that the Lord will be with me, and I shall drive them out as the Lord said.' Then Joshua blessed him and gave Hebron to Caleb . . . and the land had rest from war.

Joshua 14:6-15

We had been at a beach picnic for most of the day. Although it was January, supposedly the 'dry season', there had been much heavy rain and as we all got into our cars to leave we discovered the track was now a mud bath, impassable to a normal vehicle. One man, however, had a rugged four-wheel drive pick-up and, car by car, he towed us out of the mud. All except for one car, driven by a man who, two years previously, had sold him a fridge that didn't work! The pick-up owner had a long memory and his enemy had a long wait for rescue!

Caleb has a long memory too, but he has put his to better use. At the age of eighty-five he claims the inheritance promised him forty-five years before! The passing of time affects people differently, but it often produces a hardening of attitudes. Some, like the pick-up owner, allow the passage of years to strengthen grudges, feed grievances and produce a hardness which keeps God's power at bay. Others, like Caleb, are also hardened by years of waiting, but this hardening is more a strengthening of resolve, a determination to do God's work, to claim his promises and defeat his enemies.

What about us? Are there names and incidents from the past which have hardened to stone within us, or do the passing years only strengthen our desire to serve God? Caleb's way led to peace. Like the settlers of Canaan, God has prepared a rest for us – Caleb's way leads to it – 'and the land had rest from war'.

A prayer:

Lord God, I have been hard where I should have been soft, and soft where I should have been hard. Work in me, I pray, that the passing of time may bring me to the rest and peace you have prepared. Amen.

Wednesday: Saul can't wait

> The Philistines mustered to fight with Israel . . . Saul was still at Gilgal, and all the people followed him trembling. He waited seven days, the time appointed by Samuel; but Samuel did not come to Gilgal, and the people began to slip away from Saul. So Saul said, 'Bring the burnt offering here to me, and the offerings of well-being.' And he offered the burnt offering. As soon as he had finished offering the burnt offering, Samuel arrived; and Saul went out to meet him and salute him. Samuel said, 'What have you done?' Saul replied, 'When I saw that the people were slipping away from me, and that you did not come . . . I said, "Now the Philistines will come down upon me at Gilgal, and I have not entreated the favour of the Lord"; so I forced myself and offered the burnt offering.' Samuel said to Saul, 'You have done foolishly; you have not kept the commandment of the Lord your God, which he commanded you. The Lord would have established your kingdom over Israel forever, but now your kingdom will not continue . . .
>
> *1 Samuel 13:5, 7-15*

Not all the Old Testament characters are as worthy, or as wholehearted, as Caleb. One of the most helpful facets of Bible study is that in the pages of history, law, prophecy, poetry and wisdom we meet ourselves – all our own faults are reflected there in one character or another.

Take Saul – exceptional in so many ways and chosen as Israel's first king, but all his life plagued by fear and lack of trust. If you have known what it is to be fed up with waiting, you have been in Saul's position in this reading – the mighty Philistine army is ranged against a much weaker Israel, and Samuel is due to come and fulfil the priestly duties before battle. But the days pass and Samuel doesn't arrive so Saul goes ahead with the sacrifice, disobeying the specific commands of God that only priests should offer sacrifices. Whilst he is in the very act, Samuel turns up, horrified by Saul's disobedience and prophesying that, for this, he will lose the kingship. This marks a watershed in Saul's life, as from here things get worse and he declines further into sin, paranoia, witchcraft and fear.

All because he couldn't wait. We sympathise. In a world of increasing pressure, where information is being transmitted faster and faster every day, we too get impatient if we have to wait for things; waiting has lost its value.

An American builder, helping out on a building project in St Vincent, reported to the local foreman one morning to find out what were the jobs for that day. 'Today,' replied the foreman, 'we are waiting for the concrete to set.' 'You mean we're not doing anything?' asked the American. 'Yes, we are,' contradicted the West Indian, 'we're waiting.'

A prayer:

It isn't easy to wait, Lord God. You know how we struggle with inactivity. But how much worse is the path of disobedience and what blessings we lose by our impatience. Teach us again to wait, Lord, to wait and to trust. Amen.

Week One — Waiting

Thursday: Waiting for what?

> The days are surely coming, says the Lord, when I will
> raise up for David a righteous Branch, and he shall reign
> as king and deal wisely, and shall execute justice and
> righteousness in the land. In his days Judah will be saved
> and Israel will live in safety. And this is the name by
> which he will be called: 'The Lord is our righteousness.'
>
> *Jeremiah 23:5-6*

Waiting for what? A great deal of my life has been spent waiting for letters, for post to arrive. In rural St Vincent the daily arrival of the mail van was a highlight in the community. Those of us hopeful for letters would crowd into the tiny Post Office, packed tightly together in the heat, sweat trickling down our necks and backs, waiting and hoping that our name would be called. Oh, the disappointment when it wasn't!

Jeremiah knew more about patient waiting than most people. For forty years he preached to a hard-hearted people, faithful to the message God had given him despite mockery, suffering, abuse and exile. What was the hope that kept him going? For what was he waiting? In these verses he prophesies hope to a despairing nation. The golden age of King David is long since past and recent kings have, by their foolish alliances and lack of trust in God, led both Israel and Judah into exile. Into this situation Jeremiah brings God's words: 'The days are surely coming when I will raise up for David a righteous Branch . . .' A future king will come, of David's line, who will be wise, just and righteous, *then* Judah and Israel will be saved.

On one level Jeremiah's prophecies were fulfilled with the restoration of the exiled Jews to their homeland, but the hope he preached was realised only centuries later when a child was born in insignificant Bethlehem, born of David's line, a child who grew up and, by his death on the cross to reconcile us to God, proved that his name was indeed 'the Lord is our righteousness'.

Waiting for what? Rather, waiting for whom?

A prayer:

> *Thank you, Lord, that our waiting is not a hopeless killing of time, with no certain hope of fulfilment; rather that we can wait in quiet certainty, for you are the God who came, the God who comes and the God who will come. Amen.*

Week One — Waiting

Friday: Elizabeth

> Meanwhile the people were waiting for Zechariah, and wondered at his delay in the sanctuary. When he did come out he could not speak to them, and they realised that he had seen a vision in the sanctuary. He kept motioning to them and remained unable to speak. When his time of service was ended he went to his home. After those days his wife Elizabeth conceived, and for five months she remained in seclusion. She said, 'This is what the Lord has done for me, when he looked favourably on me and took away the disgrace I have endured among my people.'
>
> *Luke 1:21-25*

Pregnancy is also about waiting. However the news comes, whether by test, by symptoms or by angelic messenger it must be followed by months of waiting. For some these are months of health and energy; for others they are spent in the misery of nausea and exhaustion. For all there is the mixture of emotions: the joy of this intimate life growing inside, the fear and anxiety in the question 'Will my baby be okay?'

Elizabeth has already waited so long for this; like Sarah and Hannah and others before her she is considered barren, she is 'getting on in years' (Luke 1:18). We can barely imagine her mixture of emotions as her dumb husband conveys the news. There is something wonderfully Spirit-filled about everything that happens in these first two chapters of Luke and I'm always so glad that the people waiting for Zechariah to come out 'realised that he had seen a vision' — I rather suspect that if something similar happened today we would assume the minister had had a stroke and call an ambulance!

Elizabeth conceives and remains in seclusion for five months — not ashamed, for by this the Lord has taken away her perceived disgrace. No, rather we can imagine her secret joy, her irrepressible grin, her private rejoicing and her waiting . . . she's good at that. What is another nine months when you've been waiting all your life?

I have never been pregnant in Advent, although I've always felt it would be somehow appropriate, but I share, below, the thoughts of a friend who has.

A prayer

> *Thank you, Lord, for using ordinary women, ordinary wombs to bring about your great plan of salvation. May each of us, women or men, childless or parents, bear in our mortal bodies the life of Christ that we may see you brought to birth in our ordinary daily lives. Amen.*

* * * * *

LENT IN ADVENT

Weeks of preparation
and sickness
The world waits for Christmas
While I wait for wholeness
Life forming in my womb
I want to know its joy
But feel only
a set of symptoms.

Days get darker
nausea thickens
How can a shorter day
seem longer than the one before?
This greatest of blessings
brings tears
I want to leap in praise and thankfulness
Strength ebbs.

Yet isolation brings a strange comfort
Christmas stripped of parties,
company, shopping
Seems a more fitting way to prepare
For the greatest birth of all
The shadow of the cross was always there
Did Mary sense it on her way to Bethlehem?

I have great hope for the future
and trust in my God
But for me, this year
Lent came early
in Advent.

Josette Crane, December 1993

Week One – Waiting

Saturday: Zechariah – the dawn from on high

'And you, child, will be called the prophet of the
     Most High;
for you will go before the Lord to prepare his ways,
to give knowledge of salvation to his people
by the forgiveness of their sins.
By the tender mercy of our God, the dawn from on high
     will break upon us,
to give light to those who sit in darkness and in the
     shadow of death,
to guide our feet into the way of peace.'

Luke 1:76-79

The plan was simple. I would fly back from the tiny island where ten of us had been on a mission ahead of the others, who would travel later by boat. Thus I would be able to prepare the house, cook a meal, even do the laundry! But there was a technical hitch – the 'plane was delayed . . . and delayed and finally (after the boat had sailed) cancelled. I was left alone on an unfamiliar island with only a suitcase of dirty laundry, the 6am boat the next day the first chance to get back home. I rose early next morning and sat on the porch of the empty house where I had been accommodated and I watched and waited for the dawn, the dawn that would bring a boat and a return to family and friends.

At first the blackness was intense and the stars brilliant, but gradually I could make out the mountainous horizon, and a faint brightening in the sky behind which slowly increased; trees, buildings, roads took on colour and definition. Day dawned. Thank God!

The old priest Zechariah had, I feel sure, watched for the dawn many times – maybe in the fulfilment of his temple duties, maybe as he rose early to pray for the one thing he lacked – a child. Now God has amazingly, miraculously, given him a son who would become John the Baptist, and as he prophesies over his tiny baby he knows that this is the beginning of something very special.

'The dawn from on high' is about to break upon the world, and what a day that will be, bringing 'light to those who sit in darkness and in the shadow of death, to guide our feet into the way of peace'.

A prayer:

O come, thou Day-spring, come and cheer
Our spirits by thine advent here;
Disperse the gloomy clouds of night,
And death's dark shadows put to flight:
Rejoice! Rejoice! Immanuel
Shall come to thee, O Israel.

18th Century Latin
tr. John Mason Neale

Week Two — A knock in the night

Sunday: Urgent business!

Now concerning the times and the seasons, brothers and
sisters, you do not need to have anything written to you.
For you yourselves know very well that the day of the
Lord will come like a thief in the night. When they say,
'There is peace and security,' then sudden destruction will
come upon them, as labour pains come upon a pregnant
woman, and there will be no escape! But you, beloved,
are not in darkness, for that day to surprise you like a
thief; for you are all children of light and children of the
day; we are not of the night or of darkness. So then, let
us not fall asleep as others do, but let us keep awake and
be sober; for those who sleep sleep at night, and those
who are drunk get drunk at night. But since we belong to
the day, let us be sober, and put on the breastplate of
faith and love, and for a helmet the hope of salvation. For
God has destined us not for wrath but for obtaining
salvation through our Lord Jesus Christ, who died for us,
so that whether we are awake or asleep we may live with
him. Therefore encourage one another and build up each
other, as indeed you are doing.

1 Thessalonians 5:1-11

Surfacing slowly from my sleep I realised that the knocking which had
formed part of my confused dream was not a dream at all — someone,
somewhere was knocking . . . Very close, yes, just above my head,
someone was knocking at the bedroom window which was reached
from our upstairs balcony! I pulled back the curtain and saw a
woman's face, desperate, anxious. Moving to the lounge I unlocked
the patio doors and met her there. At first her rapid words in local
dialect made no sense, but finally I understood — she was pregnant,
the baby was coming, the local hospital had said she must get to the
capital. She had no transport, no money, it was 2am on a Sunday in
December — would 'Rev' take her? I woke him, he calculated that he
could do the round trip and be back in good time for his 7am service

so yes, he would, and they set off. The miles between our rural home and the capital, full of potholes, hairpin bends and heart-stopping gradients were never covered so skilfully nor so swiflty!

Some things, like babies, can't be delayed, but are urgent. In this passage (which was the set lesson for that Sunday morning's service, causing Andrew and me to exchange wry grins!) Paul writes that 'the day of the Lord' will be just such an urgent matter. There will come a time when the waiting is over and action is required. So our waiting must not become dozing. We are not to pass the time in drinking, dulling the senses, but we are to keep awake and be sober, one ear always listening, for, as the old spiritual says:

> Hush, hush, somebody's callin' my name.
> Oh my Lord, oh my Lord, what shall I do!

A prayer:

> Lord God, you know me, you know how I put off until tomorrow what can wait. Teach me, Lord, the urgency of your business, that I may recognise the time for action. Amen.

Week Two — A knock in the night

Monday: Joseph is sent for

Then the chief cupbearer said to Pharaoh, 'I remember my faults today. Once Pharaoh was angry with his servants, and put me and the chief baker in custody in the house of the captain of the guard. We dreamed on the same night, he and I, each having a dream with its own meaning. A young Hebrew was there with us, a servant of the captain of the guard. When we told him, he interpreted our dreams to us, giving an interpretation to each according to his dream. As he interpreted to us, so it turned out; I was restored to my office and the baker was hanged.' Then Pharaoh sent for Joseph, and he was hurriedly brought out of the dungeon. When he had shaved himself and changed his clothes, he came in before Pharoah. And Pharoah said to Joseph, 'I have had a dream and there is no one who can interpret it. I have heard it said of you that when you hear a dream you can interpret it.' Joseph answered Pharaoh, 'It is not I; God will give Pharaoh a favourable answer.'

Genesis 41:9-16

Some people's lives seem to follow a smooth progression, one thing leading to another in a natural, even predictable way. Joseph's life was not like that:

From the favoured son, dressed in finery, to the hated
 brother in a pit.
From a slave in chains to the chief servant in an important
 household.
From the master's favourite to the accused prisoner.

For more than two years Joseph was in jail, but just as he had at home, just as he had in Potiphar's household Joseph quickly became well-regarded and popular. There must have been an extraordinary charm about this man – a charm which Genesis 39:21 ascribes to the continuing steadfast love and favour of God. No one, except his brothers it seems, could resist showing favouritism to this one on whom God's favour, inexplicably, rested.

So, even in jail, he has reached a position of responsibility and trust. Then comes another of the disruptions to Joseph's life, the 'knock in the night'. Pharaoh has dreamed dreams and Joseph is to interpret them. Hastily he is brought from the dungeon, shaved and re-clothed to be presented to Pharaoh. Was he ready for it? Joseph has changed a lot from his rather obnoxious younger brother days. His trials have taught him much and now, as he stands before the most powerful man in the land, there is no boast on his lips about his own powers. 'It is not I, God . . .' In the crisis moment, the urgent moment, the unexpected moment, Joseph is found to be worthy, to be ready, not with his own name on his lips, but the name of God.

A prayer:

I do not know, Lord God, what this day or this night might bring, what 'knock in the night' might be just around the corner. So fill me, Lord Jesus Christ, I pray, with your Spirit that when the 'knocks' come, it will be your name that spills from my lips. Amen.

Tuesday: Passover

> At midnight the Lord struck down all the firstborn in the
> land of Egypt, from the firstborn of Pharoah who sat on
> his throne to the firstborn of the prisoner who was in the
> dungeon, and all the firstborn of the livestock. Pharoah
> arose in the night, he and all his officials and all the
> Egyptians; and there was a loud cry in Egypt, for there
> was not a house without someone dead.   Then he
> summoned Moses and Aaron in the night, and said, 'Rise
> up, go away from my people, both you and the Israelites!
> Go, worship the Lord, as you said. Take your flocks and
> your herds, as you said, and be gone.   And bring a
> blessing on me too!' . . . So the people took their dough
> before it was leavened, with their kneading bowls
> wrapped up in their cloaks on their shoulders . . . They
> baked unleavened cakes out of the dough that they had
> brought up out of Egypt; it was not leavened, because
> they were driven out of Egypt and could not wait, nor had
> they prepared any provisions for themselves.

Exodus 12:29-32, 34, 39

Four hundred years have passed since Joseph stood before
Pharoah. His family, brought to Egypt to escape famine, have
multiplied, posing a threat to the native Egyptians. This has led to
their persecution and enforced slavery but now, at last, freedom is in
the air. Yahweh has heard their cry and is acting on their behalf.
Tricks and miracles have not softened Pharaoh's heart so this is the
night of serious action. Freedom is coming, but at a price. Through
Moses and Aaron God has instructed his people in the observance of
a new festival — the Passover. Lambs are to be slaughtered and their
blood daubed on the Israelites' doorways. They are to eat hurriedly,
'your loins girded, your sandals on your feet, and your staff in your
hand' (Exodus 12:11) for this is to be a devastating 'knock in the
night'. And so, at midnight, every Egyptian family suffers a death and
suddenly, in the night, here is Pharaoh summoning Moses and Aaron,

begging them to leave, even asking for a blessing for himself. God has revealed his arm. And for the Israelites it means flight, kneading bowls and unleavened dough on their backs and the night (v42) becomes a night of vigil, firstly God's vigil, God's watching for his people, and then the people's vigil as they, as we, watch for God.

'For Christ, our Passover lamb, has been sacrificed,' Paul writes in 1 Corinthians 5:7 (NIV). The blood on the cross is for us the blood on the doorpost, and so God leads us to freedom. The Israelites had been slaves for so long. This was the night they had dreamed of, and when their chance came they were ready to take it, ready to run. Do we recognise any urgency at all in our Christian lives today or have we become complacent, content to cohabit with evil in our lives, content to remain slaves to sin, not risking all to follow Christ into full and true freedom?

A prayer:

> *Lord God, I am sorry when the leavening of the dough calls me back and slows me down, sorry for the times when I would rather enjoy the passing pleasures of the world than step with you into the freedom you have prepared for me, the freedom you died to give me. As you have watched over me, so, Lord, I watch for you in these Advent days and nights. Amen.*

Week Two – A knock in the night

Wednesday: The Lord shall suddenly come

> See, I am sending my messenger to prepare the way before me, and the Lord whom you seek will suddenly come to his temple. The messenger of the covenant in whom you delight – indeed, he is coming, says the Lord of hosts. But who can endure the day of his coming, and who can stand when he appears? For he is like a refiner's fire and like fullers' soap; he will sit as a refiner and purifer of silver, and he will purify the descendants of Levi and refine them like gold and silver, until they present offerings to the Lord in righteousness.
>
> *Malachi 3:1-3*

All-night prayer vigils are very popular among young people in parts of the Caribbean, and probably around the world. There is something exciting about gathering at night, being together in fellowship, worship and prayer through the small hours. Officially it is a night of prayer and fasting, but there will be mattresses and drinks available for those for whom the spirit is willing, but the flesh weak!

Yesterday's verses ended with the idea of 'vigil', which links into today's reading.

- The Passover *was* 'for the Lord a night of vigil, to bring them out of the land of Egypt' (Exodus 12:42); it was proof that God had been watching over them.

- The Passover was to *become* a night of vigil for all, to be kept for the Lord.

Whether officially or informally, communally or individually, whether by day or by night, we need to learn how to keep vigil, how to watch and seek, for, as Malachi prophesied four hundred years before Jesus, it is the Lord 'whom you seek' who 'will suddenly come to his temple'. It is the messenger of the covenant, 'in whom you delight' who is coming. If we are to be able to stand in that day when he comes as a refiner's fire and as fullers' soap we need to be those who, in days and nights of vigil, have sought the Lord and delighted in him. If our God is a god of our own making, a god who makes no demands on us, but fits easily into the place we have allotted to him in our lives, we may find, on that day, that it is a stranger who suddenly comes upon us.

A prayer:

> Come,' my heart says, 'seek his face!'
> Your face, Lord, do I seek.
> Do not hide your face from me. Amen.

Psalm 27:8-9

Thursday: **Thief in the night**

> But about that day and hour no one knows, neither the angels of heaven, nor the Son, but only the Father. For as the days of Noah were, so will be the coming of the Son of Man. For as in those days before the flood they were eating and drinking, marrying and giving in marriage, until the day Noah entered the ark, and they knew nothing until the flood came and swept them all away, so too will be the coming of the Son of Man. Then two will be in the field; one will be taken and one will be left. Two women will be grinding meal together; one will be taken and one will be left. Keep awake, therefore, because you do not know on what day your Lord is coming. But understand this: if the owner of the house had known in what part of the night the thief was coming, he would have stayed awake and would not have let his house be broken into. Therefore you also must be ready, for the Son of Man is coming at an unexpected hour.
>
> *Matthew 24:36-44*

'Where's the radio?' asked Andrew, wanting, as usual, to tune into the BBC World Service for the news and sport. 'Where it usually is,' I replied, but it wasn't, neither was my watch, nor the cameras . . . Gradually the truth dawned upon us – we had been burgled. Then it was that I remembered noises during the night, noises I was too tired to investigate.   Later, amusingly, came the discovery that the washing-up liquid had also gone, and a packet of cough sweets. 'Estimated value?' asked the humourless policeman! Of course, it goes without saying that we had received no notification of this beforehand, no calling card or notice of intent – surprise is all where burglary is concerned.

I find it rather strange and not a little disturbing that Jesus himself should use just such a happening, with all its shock and unpleasant aftertaste, as a picture of the coming of the Son of Man, but he does, more than once, and Paul takes it up as well. The theme of shock and surprise is wholly biblical and so we dare not be complacent.

Spanish is spoken in many islands of the Caribbean; one of the very few words I understand is the oft-repeated 'mañana', meaning 'tomorrow'. Why do today what can be left until tomorrow? The Gospel turns that philosophy on its head. 'Therefore you also must be ready, for the Son of Man is coming at an unexpected hour.' In the words of an Advent sermon of Colin Morris, 'If you have unfinished business with God, finish it now.'

A prayer:

Help me, Lord, to live this day in the light of your coming. Give me the strength to face things I am putting off; apologies I need to utter, peace I need to make, kindness I need to show and, above all, to be at peace with you that I may be ready whenever you call. Amen.

Week Two – A knock in the night

Friday: Peter is released from prison

About that time King Herod laid violent hands upon some who belonged to the church. He had James, the brother of John, killed with the sword. After he saw that it pleased the Jews, he proceeded to arrest Peter also . . . While Peter was kept in prison, the church prayed fervently for him. The very night before Herod was going to bring him out, Peter, bound with two chains, was sleeping between two soldiers, while guards in front of the door were keeping watch over the prison. Suddenly an angel of the Lord appeared and a light shone in the cell. He tapped Peter on the side and woke him, saying, 'Get up quickly.' And the chains fell off his wrists. The angel said to him, 'Fasten your belt and put on your sandals.' He did so. Then he said to him, 'Wrap your cloak around you and follow me.' Peter went out and followed him; he did not realise that what was happening with the angel's help was real; he thought he was seeing a vision.

Acts 12:1-3, 5-9

No wonder Peter thought he was seeing a vision! He must have thought this was to be his last night alive. Herod had killed James and most probably was planning the same fate for Peter. The account makes it very clear that he was heavily guarded and in chains. Yet all of this is rendered totally ineffective in the face of God's plan for his freedom. Part of Jewish belief was that all earthly religion and religious symbols were only a shadow of the reality, which was the heavenly temple. Hebrews 9 expounds this idea best. It is a belief we would do well to rediscover. Our materialistic world teaches the opposite, and even we Christians sometimes live as if reality consists of money and clothes, food and work, and as though our hope of heaven is a mere dream, our spiritual experiences only visions with no substance. 'Real, real, Christ's so real to me' we sang often in St Vincent, and one of the joys of living amongst Christians in the Caribbean has been to meet so many people to whom reality is

Jesus. As materialism advances in every part of the world, can we be people who see what is *spiritual* as eternal and real, and what is *temporal* as passing and insubstantial?

This wonderful story from Acts is a touch of heaven on earth and a reversal of all that we live by; the chains, the guards and the walls have no substance, while the angel and the vision are real! The freedom is undeniable. How ironic that, having walked out of a prison cell, Peter is then barred by the locked doors of the believers! We don't know what part their fervent prayer played in Peter's release (v12-16) but we do know that they can't believe it has been answered and so Peter's knock in the night has to go on and on! Could it be that God can deal with any obstacles placed by the enemy, but that fear and unbelief in the Christian's heart still block his purposes? Or would that be stretching the story too far?

A prayer:

> Sometimes, Lord, I catch a glimpse of your heavenly kingdom and know that to be reality, but most of the time I allow the things that I can see and touch to fool me with their apparent substance. Awaken my spirit by your Spirit that I may know your reality every moment. Amen.

Week Two – A knock in the night

Saturday: Stand and knock

> Listen! I am standing at the door, knocking; if you hear
> my voice and open the door, I will come in to you and eat
> with you, and you with me. To the one who conquers I
> will give a place with me on my throne, just as I myself
> conquered and sat down with my Father on his throne.
> Let anyone who has an ear listen to what the Spirit is
> saying to the churches.
>
> *Revelation 3:20-22*

One facet of the culture shock we experienced in leaving suburban
Britain for the rural West Indies was the manner of attracting a
household's attention. We had been brought up to stand at the door
and knock; in the North Leeward region of St Vincent the done thing
is to stand at the gate and shout! Doors may stand open anyway to
let in the breeze, the sound of knocking may be lost amongst the
noise of doors and shutters banging in the wind; most probably there
are dogs . . . so one remains on the boundary of the property and
shouts! 'Good afternoon, Mistress', 'Morning, Rev' soon became
familiar and welcome cries outside our manse at the crossroads in
Chateaubelair.

So if a Caribbean Bible were to be produced I hope this verse would
be rendered 'Listen! I stand at the gate and shout!' for the idea is the
same – it is not acceptable to enter a person's home without their
permission, the householder must make some invitation (and possibly
must tie up the dogs) before a visitor can enter. Jesus does not force
us; yes, his coming may be as *unexpected* as the thief in the night,
but he would never be that thief, he will not enter where we will not
invite him.

How far in are we prepared to invite him? In a warm climate, much
business is done in the open air. The shout at the gate might lead to
a conversation through a window, or on the porch. Rarely would I be

invited right inside a home, to see things as they were, to cope, perhaps, with cooking smells, inadequate space, flies, the everyday chaos of life . . . but also to be part of the family, sharing in highs and lows, plenty and need.

How have we responded to Jesus' shout at our gate? Opened the window? Gone out to meet him on the doorstep? Or invited him right inside to eat with us and us with him? Sometimes when Andrew was preaching in a distant village, the local folk would give him a good meal, but rarely would they sit and eat *with* him, feeling somehow that the minister should be served separately. Jesus tells us in these verses that he wants to sit and eat *with* us, our brother and friend as well as our Master and Lord.

A prayer:

> *Enter, then, O Christ most holy;*
> *Make a Christmas in my heart;*
> *Make a heaven of my manger:*
> *It is heaven where thou art. Amen.*

George Stringer Rowe

Week Three – Smoke on the mountain

Sunday: Thunder in December

On the morning of the third day there was thunder and lightning, as well as a thick cloud on the mountain, and a blast of a trumpet so loud that all the people who were in the camp trembled. Moses brought the people out of the camp to meet God. They took their stand at the foot of the mountain. Now Mount Sinai was wrapped in smoke, because the Lord had descended upon it in fire; the smoke went up like the smoke of a kiln, while the whole mountain shook violently. As the blast of the trumpet grew louder and louder, Moses would speak and God would answer him in thunder . . . Then the Lord said to Moses, 'Go down and warn the people not to break through to the Lord to look; otherwise many of them will perish.' . . . So Moses went down to the people and told them.

Exodus 19:16-19, 21, 25

The small town of Chateaubelair on St Vincent is only three miles from the foot of that island's volcano – the Soufrière – an awesome four thousand feet peak which dominates the little island. The Soufrière is still active and many eyewitnesses have told us of its most recent dramatic 'blow' on Good Friday 1979; of fireballs in the sky, of huge rocks crashing down destroying homes, of thick layers of ash covering and burning land for miles around, of evacuation, of fear, of helplessness in the face of such power. For our sisters and brothers on the island of Montserrat, the devastation and dislocation of eruption has been a recent experience.

On the third Sunday in Advent 1996 I went out on to our balcony at 5am and was surprised to see a crowd of around forty people gathered at a street corner there. I soon learned the reason – just as in the early hours of 13th April 1979 thunder had been heard, so today there had been thunder in the early hours, and thunder was not normal in December. So these folk had gathered to 'watch the mountain' – as the darkness receded and day dawned, would there be smoke? Was this thunder the forerunner of more volcanic activity? What a picture of Advent it was to see that little crowd, eyes fixed on the direction of the Soufrière, straining against the darkness for any sign. Happily, although dawn did indeed reveal a thick cloud around the mountain's peak, nothing unusual occurred and gradually the cloud, the crowd and the anxiety evaporated.

There is an awesomeness about God which we, at times, forget. The Israelites in the wilderness recognised it; for them the holiness of God was demonstrated in thunder and lightning, thick cloud, fire and smoke, and they were to keep their distance or perish. Yet they were drawn to the mountain, drawn to the power and glory of God, constantly needing warnings and reminders not to come too close, not to break through. In our Advent worship today can we rediscover the awe of God's holiness and the attraction of his glory?

A prayer:

> *Holy God, we worship you; Lord God of glory, we watch for your coming, we strain our eyes in the darkness of this world for a sign of your light breaking forth. Come, Lord Jesus. Amen.*

Week Three – Smoke on the mountain

Monday: On Mount Moriah

> After these things, God tested Abraham. He said to him,
> 'Abraham!' And he said, 'Here I am.' He said, 'Take your
> son, your only son Isaac, whom you love, and go to the
> land of Moriah, and offer him there as a burnt offering on
> one of the mountains that I shall show you.' So Abraham
> rose early in the morning, saddled his donkey, and took
> two of his young men with him, and his son Isaac; he cut
> the wood for the burnt offering and set out . . . When they
> came to the place that God had shown him, Abraham built
> an altar there and laid the wood in order. He bound his
> son Isaac, and laid him on the altar, on top of the wood.
> Then Abraham reached out his hand and took the knife to
> kill his son. But the angel of the Lord called to him from
> heaven and said, 'Abraham, Abraham!' And he said,
> 'Here I am.' He said, 'Do not lay your hand on the boy or
> do anything to him; for now I know that you fear God,
> since you have not withheld your son, your only son, from
> me.'
>
> *Genesis 22:1-3, 9-12*

One thing that surprises me about this story is that in this whole
chapter, this remarkable, dramatic incident which speaks to us on so
many levels, we are not given any window into Abraham's emotions.
There is no pleading, no begging God to change his mind, there is no
outpouring of relief at the stay of execution. Why did Abraham, who
was willing to irritate God by his persistent pleading for the residents
of Sodom and Gomorrah in Genesis 18, not object to God's demand?
Why did he not point out the unreasonableness of it, remind God that
Isaac was the child of the promise, the living proof of God's covenant
purposes? Why did he obey at all?

Faith? Of course. Of course Abraham had great faith, legendary
faith, and the writer to the Hebrews ascribes his obedience to his
remarkable faith in God (Hebrews 11:17-19). Faith that God could

still work out his purposes, even without Isaac. Faith too, perhaps, that God knew what was best for him, for Abraham. Did Abraham know, in his heart of hearts, that his love for Isaac was beginning to threaten his love for God? Was his absorption in the boy undermining his wholehearted devotion to his Lord? Whether or not that was true for Abraham I believe it is true for many of us that at some point in our lives something – a relationship, money, a job, a skill – threatens to take first place and then God may have to take drastic action and raise the knife; not to prove to *himself* where our devotion lies, but to prove it to *us*. And God does not ask Abraham, or us, to do anything he will not do himself, for – in Michael Card's words – 'What Abraham was asked to do, he has done; He's offered his only Son.'

Abraham's emotions are hidden from us, but we can imagine how he felt as he released Isaac, killed the ram and laid the coals to the wood at last (v13-14) in a sacrifice of praise, relief, thanksgiving and, perhaps, repentance. And with Abraham's heart pure before God how sweet was the smoke on the mountain that day.

A prayer:

> *Search me, O God, and know my heart; test me and know my thoughts. See if there is any wicked way in me, and lead me in the way everlasting.*
>
> *Psalm 139:23-24*

Week Three – Smoke on the mountain

Tuesday: Elijah and the prophets of Baal

> So Ahab sent to all the Israelites and assembled the prophets at Mount Carmel. Elijah then came near to all the people and said, 'How long will you go limping with two different opinions? If the Lord is God, follow him; but if Baal, then follow him.' The people did not answer him a word. Then Elijah said to the people, 'I, even I only, am left a prophet of the Lord; but Baal's prophets number four hundred and fifty. Let two bulls be given to us; let them choose one bull for themselves, cut it in pieces, and lay it on the wood, but put no fire to it; I will prepare the other bull and lay it on the wood, but put no fire to it. Then you call on the name of your god and I will call on the name of the Lord; the god who answers by fire is indeed God.' All the people answered, 'Well spoken!'

1 Kings 18:20-24

Today we gather on a third mountain top, Mount Carmel on the Mediterranean coast, not far, in fact, from Nazareth in Galilee. What a drama unfolds before our eyes as we spend the day there in the company of Elijah, four hundred and fifty prophets of Baal and 'all the people'. Read the full story in 1 Kings 18:20-40. Elijah is on top form, so zealous for God that he doesn't even mind sounding a bit self-righteous! Baal's prophets too are in full voice, calling on the name of Baal all day, crying aloud, limping, raving, cutting themselves, bleeding. Two parties, however, remain silent; the people, who, challenged by Elijah to choose whom to serve, find nothing to say and Baal from whom, despite all the efforts of his prophets, there is silence.

Imagine the glee in Elijah's face as he takes his turn; the totally superfluous action of drenching the bull and the wood – what a showman he is! But not, it seems, in his prayers. In contrast to the noisy supplications of his opponents he speaks a couple of sentences and fire falls. The smoke on the mountain proclaims that God is God indeed and the people, finding their voices, fall on their faces.

As a family, we have tried to light bonfires on beaches and failed; we have had barbecues where only the firelighters would burn, we have had barbecues where even the firelighters wouldn't burn; we have felt something of the despair of these pagan prophets!

As a Christian church around the world we have had revival campaigns that came to nothing, stewardship reviews that didn't catch on, crusades where nobody was saved; we have felt something of the despair of these pagan prophets!

Yes, there are times when we simply have to remain faithful in the face of apparent defeat, but let our prayer always be that God is seen to be God in his world today.

A prayer:

> *Answer me, O Lord, answer me, so that this people may know that you, O Lord, are God, and that you have turned their hearts back. Amen.*
>
> *1 Kings 18:37*

Week Three – Smoke on the mountain

Wednesday: The mountain of the Lord

> In days to come the mountain of the Lord's house shall be established as the highest of the mountains, and shall be raised up above the hills. People shall stream to it, and many nations shall come and say: 'Come, let us go up to the mountain of the Lord, to the house of the God of Jacob; that he may teach us his ways and that we may walk in his paths.' For out of Zion shall go forth instruction, and the word of the Lord from Jerusalem. He shall judge between many peoples, and shall arbitrate between strong nations far away; they shall beat their swords into ploughshares, and their spears into pruning hooks; nation shall not lift up sword against nation, neither shall they learn war any more; but they shall sit under their own vines and under their own fig trees, and no one shall make them afraid; for the mouth of the Lord of hosts has spoken.
>
> *Micah 4:1-4*

On holiday on Union Island, one of the string of little gems between St Vincent and Grenada, we decided to climb 'the Pinnacle', a thousand feet peak, the top section of which was more or less bare rock. It was not an easy climb for several reasons: there was no clear path – at the foot of the mountain there were too many paths, aimless sheep tracks which took us nowhere; higher up there were no paths at all.   The 'bush' (vegetation) was extremely hostile – we encountered 'burn bush' which has to be felt to be believed; cacti abounded and Andrew was stung by a 'Jack Spaniard', less aggressive but much more painful than an ordinary wasp. Having two small boys of almost six and almost two didn't make things any easier either, and it was very, very hot, the middle of a tropical day.

Why persevere? There is something compulsive about mountain climbing, isn't there? At one thousand feet this was barely a mountain, but it was the biggest there was and we wanted to gain that high ground, to be on top of the world. Eventually we made it, and as we perched on the rocky summit and surveyed the land we felt that we had conquered! Towns and villages lay like toys beneath us, boats lay at anchor in tiny harbours, coral reefs glowed white through the turquoise waters around us, other islands dotted the sea and more distant islands with their peaks pushed up the horizon. Even mistakes we had made in our route were now clearly visible! Timothy voiced the question in all our minds, 'I don't know how we're going to get down again,' but it was great to be there, worth the effort, the pain, the frustration, the sweat, the tears.

The Christian way is often hard to find and often thorny. We meet many obstacles and may, at times, feel encumbered by the needs of fellow travellers, but our goal is worth it. The mountain of the Lord will be established, and I am determined to be there.

A prayer:

> *Travelling God, travel with us on life's journey, teach us your ways that we may walk in your paths, today and as long as we live. Amen.*

Thursday: The Transfiguration

And while he was praying, the appearance of his face changed, and his clothes became dazzling white. Suddenly they saw two men, Moses and Elijah, talking to him. They appeared in glory and were speaking of his departure, which he was about to accomplish at Jerusalem. Now Peter and his companions were weighed down with sleep; but since they had stayed awake, they saw his glory and the two men who stood with him. Just as they were leaving him, Peter said to Jesus, 'Master, it is good for us to be here; let us make three dwellings, one for you, one for Moses, and one for Elijah' − not knowing what he said. While he was saying this, a cloud came and overshadowed them; and they were terrified as they entered the cloud. Then from the cloud came a voice that said, 'This is my Son, my Chosen; listen to him!' When the voice had spoken, Jesus was found alone. And they kept silent and in those days told no one any of the things they had seen.

Luke 9:29-36

Moses and Elijah, two great mountaineers from the Old Testament, both probably thought they had had their greatest 'mountain-top experiences', Moses at Sinai, Elijah at Carmel. But to them is given this tremendous moment, to see God face to face in the transfigured face of Jesus. And not to them alone, for our three sleepy friends are there too; Peter, James and John, still struggling to keep pace with their extraordinary Master, *just manage* to stay sufficiently awake to see the glory of God in the face of Christ!

Sleep is one of God's greatest gifts. In Britain people tend to be a little bit apologetic about sleeping; it doesn't fit in too well with the work ethic! In the Caribbean, I'm glad to say, people unashamedly enjoy sleeping. The capacity for hard work is enormous and is matched by an equal capacity for plenty of sleep!

Some things, however, are not to be missed, even for sleep. It would be a dull Carnival if revellers were not prepared to forgo sleep for days at a time, catching up later when the fun is over. How thankful we must be that Peter, James and John kept awake for this momentous experience. Moses and Elijah, the law and the prophets, meet with the fulfilment of both in the incarnate God, Jesus Christ. What did they talk of, those three? Luke tells us they talked of Jesus' departure, literally his exodus, which he was about to accomplish at Jerusalem.

On an unnamed mountain, these three who had scaled the heights for God, literally and spiritually, discussed what was soon to happen on a nearby hilltop, for that would be the fulfilment of the work of all three of them. No smoke in this mountain story, but a thick cloud overshadows them all, God speaks and, like the disciples, we are left in awe at the greatness of God.

A prayer:

> *Wake us up, Lord, from the sleep which weighs upon our souls and prevents us from seeing your glory. As the cloud rolls back, may we see you alone, for in you is our hope of glory. Amen.*

Friday: The Morning Star

> For we did not follow cleverly devised myths when we made known to you the power and coming of our Lord Jesus Christ, but we had been eyewitnesses of his majesty. For he received honour and glory from God the Father when the voice was conveyed to him by the Majestic Glory, saying, 'This is my Son, my Beloved, with whom I am well pleased.' We ourselves heard this voice come from heaven, while we were with him on the holy mountain. So we have the prophetic message more fully confirmed. You will do well to be attentive to this as to a lamp shining in a dark place, until the day dawns and the morning star rises in your hearts. First of all you must understand this, that no prophecy of scripture is a matter of one's own interpretation, because no prophecy ever came by human will, but men and women moved by the Holy Spirit spoke from God.
>
> *2 Peter 1:16-21*

Some years after the experience of yesterday's reading, Peter writes of that day in his Second Letter. Before he dies, Peter wants to make his bequest to the Christians of his day and, thank God, to us. James is (probably) dead already, and only John and Peter remain to tell the story of that unforgettable day when they were eyewitnesses of Christ's majesty. Peter's language is superlative, over the top, as he tells us again and again. 'This really happened, don't doubt that Jesus Christ is God.'

Peter, the working fisherman, can now handle words as competently as he handles nets as he challenges us to 'be attentive to this as to a lamp shining in a dark place, until the day dawns and the morning star rises in your heart'. As a fisherman he too would have known many dawns and watched many times for the rising of the morning star, signalling the time to end the night's work and go home to rest. This picture he translates into the spiritual realm; of the darkness around he has much to say in the remainder of his letter, but whatever happens, however many faithful apostles are put to the sword, there is a lamp burning, the lamp of the light of Christ's glory, and it is to this that we are to be attentive.

How, during this Advent season can we be attentive to God, how, as the season gets busier and Christmas approaches, can we make sure we are preparing to let Christ in, not to shut him out? As the hours of daylight get shorter, (whether materially so in Britain, or less noticeably in the Caribbean), we must train our inner eyes on the light of Christ; as we seek to dispel the darkness by candle, oil lamp or electric light to give ourselves more time for all there is to do, we must also come to the true light in praise and adoration.

A prayer:

> *Christ is the morning star who, when the night of this world is past, brings to his saints the promise of the light of life and opens everlasting day. Amen.*
>
> *Bede*

Week Three — Smoke on the mountain

Saturday: You have come to Mount Zion

> You have not come to something that can be touched, a blazing fire, and darkness, and gloom, and a tempest, and the sound of a trumpet, and a voice whose words made the hearers beg that not another word be spoken to them. (For they could not endure the order that was given, 'If even an animal touches the mountain, it shall be stoned to death.' Indeed so terrifying was the sight that Moses said, 'I tremble with fear.') But you have come to Mount Zion and to the city of the living God, the heavenly Jerusalem, and to innumerable angels in festal gatherings, and to the assembly of the firstborn who are enrolled in heaven, and to God the judge of all, and to the spirits of the righteous made perfect, and to Jesus the mediator of a new covenant, and to the sprinkled blood that speaks a better word than the blood of Abel.
>
> *Hebrews 12:18-24*

As this third week in Advent draws to a close, the writer to the Hebrews takes us back in thought to where we began the week. In this commentary on Exodus 19, we are taken from the physical Mount Sinai to the spiritual Mount Zion. Mount Zion, that symbolic mountain which has in it something of Mount Sinai, something of Mount Carmel, something of the mountain of transfiguration and even of Calvary's hill. Mount Zion which, to the geographer or map-maker doesn't exist at all, but which, to the believer, is more real than Everest, Ben Nevis or the Soufrière!

We are back to the Hebrew idea that what is really real cannot be touched, cannot be shaken (v27). God's final shaking, like a powerful threshing to separate the grain from the chaff, like a mighty refining which removes the dross from the gold, will remove *all* created things. Only those things which cannot be shaken will remain and those who survive will receive a kingdom that cannot be shaken (v28).

What is there about my Christmas preparations or yours which cannot be shaken? Gifts and cards will not last, but if they are given in love, that will endure; food and drink is all too quickly consumed at Christmas as every cook knows, but the warmth of hospitality lasts and kindness to a stranger or a lonely person may be remembered forever. Tinsel has to be packed away, Christmas trees die, fairy lights fuse and wear out (usually on Christmas Eve!) but the wonder in a child's eyes can set the feet upon the road to Mount Zion. With less than a week to go, let us make sure we have built into our Christmas celebrations something that cannot be shaken.

A prayer:

There's a light upon the mountains,
and the day is at the spring,
When our eyes shall see the beauty and the
glory of the King;
Weary was our heart with waiting, and the
night-watch seemed so long;
But his triumph-day is breaking, and we hail it
with a song. Amen.

Henry Burton

Week Four – The 'plane now landing

Sunday: A special visit

When the queen of Sheba heard of the fame of Solomon, (fame due to the name of the Lord), she came to test him with hard questions. She came to Jerusalem with a very great retinue, with camels bearing spices, and very much gold, and precious stones; and when she came to Solomon, she told him all that was on her mind. Solomon answered all her questions; there was nothing hidden from the king that he could not explain to her. When the queen of Sheba had observed all the wisdom of Solomon . . . there was no more spirit in her. So she said to the king, 'The report was true that I heard in my own land of your accomplishments and of your wisdom, but I did not believe the reports until I came and my own eyes had seen it. Not even half had been told me; your wisdom and prosperity far surpass the report that I had heard . . . Blessed be the Lord your God who has delighted in you and set you on the throne of Israel! Because the Lord loved Israel forever, he has made you king to execute justice and righteousness. Then she gave the king one hundred and twenty talents of gold, a great quantity of spices, and precious stones; never again did spices come in such quantity as that which the queen of Sheba gave to King Solomon.

1 Kings 10:1-7, 9-10

In the small island communities of the South Caribbean *everyone* has family overseas. Children have travelled to Britain to study, cousins have emigrated to the United States or Canada to work, brothers and sisters have moved to larger islands where there are more opportunities. For us, 4,000 miles from 'home', *all* our family is overseas. Letters are a real blessing, 'phone calls are precious, photos and videos exchanged mark the growth of grandchildren and are treasured, but the excitement really mounts when someone has scraped together the air fare and tells us, 'I'm coming to see you.' Waiting at airports, watching screens for news of arrival times, scanning the horizon for the dot which may turn into the 'plane which may be bringing a grandparent, a sister, a friend . . . these are part of small island living. And then, when the 'plane finally lands, when the immigration and customs officers are finally satisfied, then come the hugs and kisses and the non-stop talking, the depth of intimacy and communication which even the best letters can't convey.

The queen of Sheba too knew the gap between reports and reality: 'Not even the half had been told me.' In her visit to Solomon, the stories she had heard took on flesh, and there was an incarnation. Every 'plane that lands here at Point Salines Airport, Grenada, bringing family and friends to visit someone is an incarnation, the best possible way of communicating. On this last Sunday in Advent, the excitement is mounting, the preparations are in full swing, the 'plane is getting very close, it is almost ready to land . . .

A prayer:

Open our eyes, Lord Jesus, to be dazzled by your splendour and to see in the humble baby in the stall such riches and wisdom as leave us short of breath. Amen.

Week Four — The 'plane now landing

Monday: The Word is very near to you

> Surely, this commandment that I am commanding you today is not too hard for you, nor is it too far away. It is not in heaven, that you should say, 'Who will go up to heaven for us, and get it for us, so that we may hear it and observe it?' Neither is it beyond the sea, that you should say, 'Who will cross to the other side of the sea for us, and get it for us so that we may hear it and observe it?' No, the word is very near to you; it is in your mouth and in your heart for you to observe.
>
> *Deuteronomy 30:11-14*

As a parent of young children I issue a lot of commands, too many probably. Most of these, I hope, are to safeguard my children's health and safety, to promote sound values or to keep the home a peaceful place. Some, I have to confess, are to preserve my own sanity. Some are easy for the boys to obey, others are hard, a few are probably impossible. When commands are not kept, punishment has to follow in order for the command to be valued. Sometimes the punishment comes as a natural consequence of disobedience, sometimes it is enforced. This whole process, known to all parents, is one of the most tedious aspects of rearing children; how we wish we could somehow implant in our offspring both the desire and the strength to be obedient. How we long for the day when they will see for themselves what is right and good, and will choose to follow that way.

'Surely,' says God to his people, 'this commandment is not too hard . . . nor is it too far away . . . No, the word is very near to you.' Like a parent trying to discipline a child, God struggled for generations with a disobedient people, but throughout the Old Testament we are given hints that there is a better way. Jeremiah prophesies, 'I will put my law within them and I will write it on their hearts' (31:33). Further on in this chapter of Deuteronomy we read that the way to obey the commandments is to love (v16). In other words, our relationship with

God is not meant to be an external one, shown in the keeping of rules, but an internal one, for the laws that God gives are to be placed within us. 'No,' says God, 'the word is very near to you'.

As Christmas week begins, the Word is indeed very near to us, wanting to be born in our hearts, wanting to fill our lives with his life. We don't need to go up to heaven for this Word, nor cross the sea to seek him, for this Living Word came down to us!

A prayer:

> *For too long I have lived as a disobedient child, at times frustrated by my own rebellion, at times trying to evade your commands. Thank you, Lord God, that you have sent your Word to dwell within me, to change me from the inside. Amen.*

Week Four – The 'plane now landing

Tuesday: Ages ago I was set up

> The Lord created me at the beginning of his work,
>   the first of his acts of long ago.
> Ages ago I was set up, at the first, before the
>   beginning of the earth.
> When there were no depths I was brought forth,
> When there were no springs abounding with water.
> Before the mountains had been shaped, before the
>   hills, I was brought forth . . .
> . . . Then I was beside him like a master worker;
>   and I was daily his delight,
> rejoicing before him always,
> rejoicing in his inhabited world and delighting in
>   the human race.
>
> *Proverbs 8:21-25, 30-31*

Mystery lies at the heart of Christmas. When my young nephews wanted facts about Father Christmas, my sister, faced with the difficult choice between a lie or disillusionment, would smile and say, 'There are a lot of mysteries at Christmas.' How true! Thank God for mystery, for wonder, for things we can't explain, analyse or prove. Yet we need to grapple with the mysteries, secure in the knowledge that we will never solve them, and exhilarated by the attempt.

One of the central mysteries of Christian belief is the relationship between God and Jesus; even young children sense this: 'Who looked after the world when Jesus died?' 'How could God be a baby?' Sometimes theologians give very clumsy names to very thrilling truths; we may close our ears to talk of the 'pre-incarnate Christ', but how wonderful to read the whole of this passage from Proverbs and to hear Jesus speaking, from hundreds of years before his birth in Bethlehem. The Wisdom, the Word of God, was first to be created, to be 'set up', to be 'brought forth', from what? It can only be from God himself. God is not a loner, he delights in society, in company, 'and I was daily his delight'. Together the Lord and his master worker rejoiced in the people they had made, 'delighting in the human race'.

We are in danger of undermining the essence of Christmas if we call it a birthday party and celebrate it simply as an anniversary. 'Before Abraham was, I AM,' Jesus told the Jews (John 8:58); it almost led to his being stoned, for such mysteries are hard to accept. They may not fit with the pictures we have grown up with, they may stretch our minds uncomfortably, but they are vital if we are, this Christmas, to stand in awe at what God has done.

A prayer:

> *O Christ, the Wisdom and the Word of God, I bow before you in worship and praise, for wisdom is better than jewels and all that I desire cannot compare with you. Amen.*

Week Four – The 'plane now landing

Wednesday: God has spoken by his Son

> Long ago God spoke to our ancestors in many and various ways by the prophets, but in these last days he has spoken to us by a Son, whom he appointed heir of all things, through whom he also created the worlds. He is the reflection of God's glory and the exact imprint of God's very being, and he sustains all things by his powerful word. When he had made purification for sins, he sat down at the right hand of the Majesty on high, having become as much superior to angels as the name he has inherited is more excellent than theirs.
>
> *Hebrews 1:1-4*

In the rural North Leeward area of St Vincent, communication combines some of the best elements of modern technology with the ancient charms of the 'bush telegraph'. As a minister's wife, I frequently had to try and get a message to a husband who might be anywhere! I would start with 'phone calls to persons at strategic points of his possible routes, houses and bars on street corners where people may sit all day, making just the kind of study of passing traffic I needed: 'Have you seen Rev's car pass yet?' Infallibly he would be tracked down and the message delivered – who needs a mobile 'phone in Chateaubelair?

In some ways the Bible is a record of the messages God has been seeking to give us since the days of our creation. At first, Hebrews tells us, he spoke by the prophets, but now, in these last days, by a Son.

Messengers, however reliable, are not always believed. When I received a message that my husband's return flight to Grenada from Carriacou was to arrive an hour early I didn't believe it. Although the local interpretation of the airline's name, LIAT, was Leave Islands Any Time, this had never, in my experience, meant a 'plane leaving *before* schedule. As the representative on the airline's desk didn't believe it either I took the children off to the beach instead and only by a minor miracle did we spot Andrew setting off to walk home!

Messengers from God are not always believed either, particularly when their message is unlikely and so God sends his Son. Jesus not only brings the message, he *is* the message, for this is an important message, one that God does not want to be misunderstood or ignored. It is this message that we celebrate this week.

A prayer:

Lord God, you have gone to extraordinary lengths to reach us with your message. This Christmas I open my ears to your voice, my mind to your ways, my eyes to your glory, my heart to your love. Amen.

Week Four – The 'plane now landing

Thursday: 'Coming – ready or not!'

> In the time of King Herod, after Jesus was born in Bethlehem of Judea, magi from the East came to Jersualem, asking, 'Where is the child who has been born king of the Jews? For we observed his star at its rising, and have come to pay him homage.' . . . When they had heard the king, they set out; and there, ahead of them, went the star that they had seen at its rising, until it stopped over the place where the child was. When they saw that the star had stopped, they were overwhelmed with joy.
>
> *Matthew 2:1-2, 9-10*

Some people, perhaps especially in the UK and similar cultures, like to plan everything well in advance. The summer holiday is booked in January, or earlier, the Christmas shopping is done as soon as the summer holiday is over. A diary is vital to keep all those forward plans in order, and the loss of the diary comes as a fatal blow!

Life in the Caribbean is, generally, not like that. Few people live by a diary, so meetings can be arranged at very short notice. Even major events are only publicised a week or two ahead. When visiting England now, I am surprised to see posters advertising events that are still months ahead. Of course, both systems have their bonuses, and their frustrations.

As we look at the Christmas story, we can see both these approaches mirrored in the leading characters. The shepherds knew nothing of what was to come and had made no preparations. For them the gathering in the stable was very much a surprise party. The magi, on the other hand, had been preparing for months, maybe years. They, through careful watching, had seen the star of Jesus 'at its rising' and their arrival at the home of Mary, Joseph and Jesus was the culmination of much thought, planning, seeking and journeying.

Can we combine the best in both the magi and the shepherds as we celebrate this Christmas? Throughout the season of Advent we have been on a journey, travelling step by step, prayer by prayer, towards the moment of revelation so nearly upon us. But we need not worry overmuch if we've forgotten to buy Brussels sprouts or sorrel*, or if we haven't had time to make new curtains or dozens of mince pies; like the shepherds we can still rush, amazed and rejoicing, to worship the Christ.

A prayer:

> *You, O Lord, have set my feet upon this journey of discovery and I am overwhelmed by joy. You, O Lord, have crashed into my darkness with your light and I rejoice. Come, Lord Jesus. Amen.*

*The red sepals of the tropical plant sorrel are infused with spices to make a traditional dark red Christmas drink, loved throughout the Caribbean.

Friday: Up and down

> And Mary said,
> 'My soul magnifies the Lord, and my spirit rejoices in God
>   my Saviour,
> for he has looked with favour on the lowliness of his
>   servant . . .
> He has brought down the powerful from their thrones,
> and lifted up the lowly;
> He has filled the hungry with good things, and sent the
> rich away empty.'
>
> *Luke 1:46-48, 52-53*

'It's not fair' is a frequent cry on the lips of most children, reflecting, perhaps, that justice is a deep human need. Of course, a child's concept of justice is limited and self-centred – it's not fair if my brother doesn't wash up as much as I do, but it's quite acceptable for someone else to tidy away all my toys!

Justice is also a thread running throughout Scripture and one which surfaces here in Mary's great song of praise – the coming of Jesus is to restore balance in the world. Like a see-saw, one end (the powerful) needs to go down if the other end (the lowly) is to be lifted up. Did Mary think of her words again when rough, humble shepherds were able to gaze into the eyes of God himself, or when wealthy foreign dignitaries knelt down and paid homage to the child of a poor family?

Developed societies tend to associate wealth simply with money or resources, but in fact real wealth has many facets: education, opportunity, family life, secure relationships, spirituality, compassion – in all these and more we can be wealthy or impoverished. The coming of Jesus challenges us to do some balancing work ourselves. If we are at the top of that see-saw perhaps we need to climb down and do something this Christmas to raise up someone who is at the other end.

A prayer:

I am sorry, Lord, that too often I accept the status quo, that your yearning for justice passes me by. Scatter my pride that I may work with you in your great balancing work. Amen.

Week Four – The 'plane now landing

Christmas Eve: The birth

In those days a decree went out from Emperor Augustus that all the world should be registered. This was the first registration and was taken while Quirinius was Governor of Syria. All went to their own towns to be registered. Joseph also went from the town of Nazareth in Galilee to Judea, to the city of David called Bethlehem, because he was descended from the house and family of David. He went to be registered with Mary to whom he was engaged and who was expecting a child. While they were there, the time came for her to deliver her child. And she gave birth to her firstborn son and wrapped him in bands of cloth, and laid him in a manger, because there was no place for them in the inn.

Luke 2:1-7

Christmas Eve is always my favourite day of the whole year. Most of the work is done, just the mince pies to make while listening to the Festival of Nine Lessons and Carols from King's College, Cambridge . . . lights sparkling, candles glowing, maybe a Christingle service in the late afternoon, or a few friends in before going to Midnight Communion, stockings, stuffing, sprouts, anticipation . . .

It isn't like that in the Caribbean and I've had to do some adjusting! Christmas Eve, for many, is the worst day of the year. Up before dawn to search out meat from neighbours or friends who may have killed a pig or cow, cleaning the house from top to bottom, making new curtains, even whitewashing the walls, all has to be done on Christmas Eve.

We wanted to hold services. 'On Christmas Eve? No way, Rev!'. We invited all the congregations to the manse for carols and mince pies, and seven people came . . .! The World Service could just about connect me with Cambridge, but there were many gremlins!

Adjusting hasn't been easy and I've resisted much of it, still wanting to keep Christmas Eve as a holy, special day.

But as I read today's passage and reflect on Mary, I wonder if the West Indian way isn't closer to the truth. There was no romanticising, no sentimentality, no gentle, traditional relaxation for Mary on that first Christmas Eve. Instead there was an arduous journey, a desperate search for lodgings, and the agony of labour.

But just as we must not lose the reality in the trappings, so we must not lose the wonder in the work, for every mother knows that after the pain comes unspeakable awe and joy. After Mary had first received the news of what was to be and had accepted it (Luke 1:26-38) Luke tells us that 'the angel left her' and for nine difficult months she walked by faith. Now the Lord is with her and, exhausted as she must have been, I believe Mary really celebrated that first, holy Christmas, overshadowed by the power of the Most High.

A prayer:

> In work or relaxation, in busy-ness or quietness, in company or solitude, overshadow us by your power today, O Lord Most High, that in awe and wonder we may see your holiness born amongst us. Amen.

Week Four – The 'plane now landing

Christmas Day: The Word became flesh

> In the beginning was the Word, and the Word was with God, and the Word was God. He was in the beginning with God. All things came into being through him, and without him not one thing came into being. What has come into being in him was life, and the life was the light of all people. The light shines in the darkness, and the darkness did not overcome it. There was a man sent from God whose name was John. He came as a witness to testify to the light, so that all might believe through him. He himself was not the light, but he came to testify to the light. The true light, which enlightens everyone, was coming into the world. He was in the world, and the world came into being through him; yet the world did not know him. He came to what was his own, and his own people did not accept him. But to all who received him, who believed in his name, he gave power to become children of God, who were born, not of blood or of the will of the flesh or of the will of man, but of God. And the Word became flesh and lived among us, and we have seen his glory, the glory as of a father's only son, full of grace and truth.

> *John 1:1-14*

For thirteen verses we can almost hear John thinking, 'Dare I say it?' He begins his Gospel with a beautiful eulogy to the Word, a passage which has been admired for its style and truth throughout the ages. He begins to 'earth' it all in v6 with a reference to John the Baptist. By v10 he is dropping broad hints of something more and finally in v14 he spits it out, *'And the Word became flesh.'* The words are familiar to us and perhaps we find it hard to imagine how some of his original readers would have recoiled at them, for, to the Greek mind, such a statement was anathema. Word was Word and flesh was flesh, Word was good and flesh was bad, Word was light and flesh was dark, Word was pure and flesh was corrupt. How, then, could Word become flesh?

How indeed? What happened in a stable in Bethlehem, two thousand years ago was not the birth of a great man, a leader, a teacher, a preacher, a philanthropist; what happened was the clothing of God in human flesh. This was God saying, 'I'll go myself'. So many sects and religious groups have fallen short because they cannot accept this, that Jesus Christ was fully God and fully human. We cannot understand or grasp it, but we must believe it.

This is the Incarnation, this is the fulfilment of Genesis and Exodus, of Deuteronomy and Samuel, of Kings and Psalms, of Proverbs and Isaiah, of Jeremiah and Malachi. This day stands alongside Good Friday and Easter Day as days without equal in the history of the universe. As the English pop group, 'Queen' sang, 'On this one Day of days, thank God it's Christmas.'

A prayer:

> *Stand amazed, ye heavens, at this!*
> *See the Lord of earth and skies;*
> *Humbled to the dust he is,*
> *And in a manger lies.*

> *Charles Welsey*